# TODAY'S WORL

# THE WORLD OF THE
# ATOM

**NEIL ARDLEY**

SHOOTING STAR PRESS

# CONTENTS

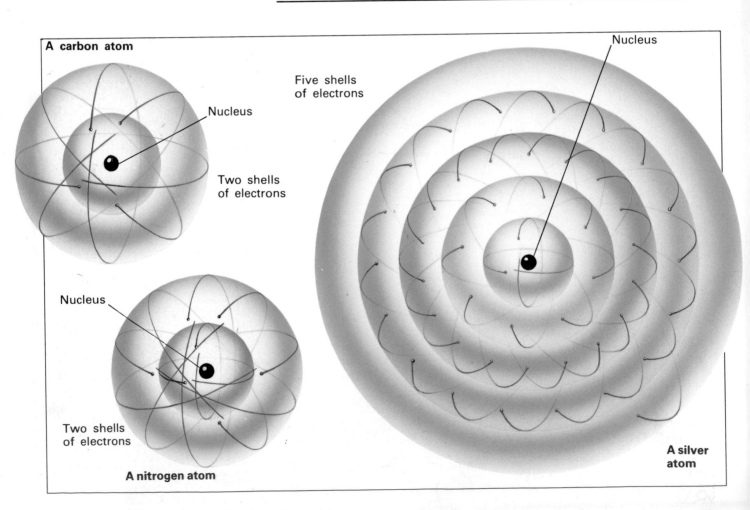

A carbon atom

Nucleus

Two shells of electrons

Nucleus

Two shells of electrons

A nitrogen atom

Five shells of electrons

Nucleus

A silver atom

# INTRODUCTION

If you have good eyesight, the smallest thing you can see is a speck of dust or a tiny grain of sand. Using a powerful microscope, we can see things as small as bacteria, the invisible germs that cause disease. And with an electron microscope, scientists can study viruses – disease-causing organisms so small that several million of them could be crowded onto a pinhead.

Yet viruses are still not the smallest things there are. The chemicals that make up viruses are themselves made of molecules, and molecules in turn are composed of even smaller atoms. So is an atom the smallest thing there is? The answer to this question is no, because atoms also have a structure and are built up from subatomic particles such as protons and electrons.

Nevertheless, everything in the universe is composed of atoms or parts of them. Ninety-two different kinds of atoms occur naturally on Earth, and more than a dozen others have been made artificially. Chemistry is the science that studies the structure of atoms and how they react and behave.

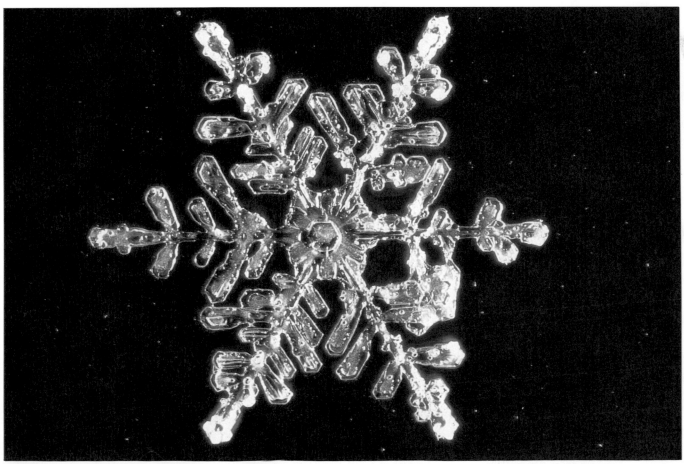

Close-up of a snowflake, consisting of water molecules arranged as a hexagonal crystal

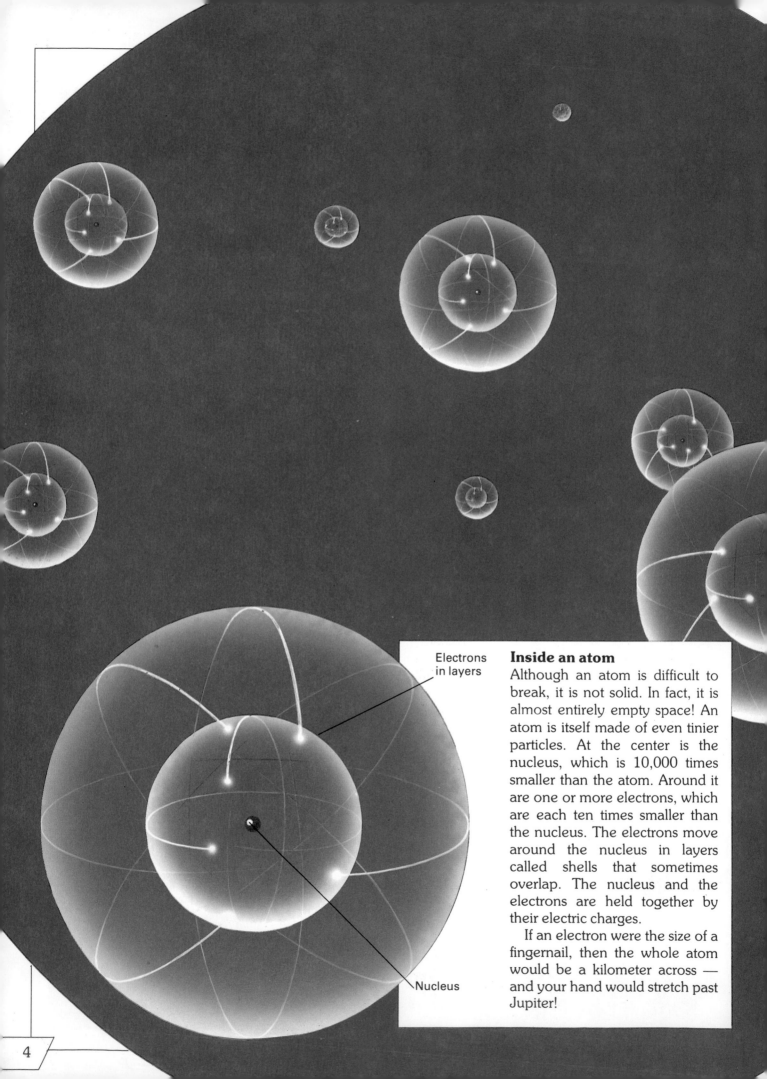

Electrons
in layers

**Inside an atom**
Although an atom is difficult to break, it is not solid. In fact, it is almost entirely empty space! An atom is itself made of even tinier particles. At the center is the nucleus, which is 10,000 times smaller than the atom. Around it are one or more electrons, which are each ten times smaller than the nucleus. The electrons move around the nucleus in layers called shells that sometimes overlap. The nucleus and the electrons are held together by their electric charges.

If an electron were the size of a fingernail, then the whole atom would be a kilometer across — and your hand would stretch past Jupiter!

Nucleus

# ATOMS EVERYWHERE

## The size of atoms

Atoms are so small that if you could line them up side by side, then fifty million atoms would measure only a centimeter. This page is about a million atoms thick.

A million is such a huge number that it's difficult to get an idea of the actual size of an atom. However, imagine that every atom in your body were the size of a fingernail. You would then be so big that you could hold the whole world in your hands!

**Size of atom:**
1/50,000,000 cm
1/20,000,000 in.

**Thickness of this page:**
1/50 cm (1/20 in.)

**Your height:**
About 150 cm (59 in.)

**Diameter of the Earth:**
1,270,000,000 cm
(500,000,000 in.)

What's inside things? Imagine that you could cut something up into tiny pieces. Could you keep on cutting forever so that the pieces would keep on getting smaller and smaller?

The answer is no. Eventually, you would have very many tiny particles that could not be cut up any more. These particles are called atoms, a word that means "uncuttable." Atoms are very small indeed. Just one grain of salt, which is probably the smallest thing in your home, contains many billions of atoms.

Everything – your body and all living things, the whole world and all the other planets – is made of atoms. Inside any object, there are many, many atoms linked together. However, there are only just over a hundred different kinds of atoms. Salt and water, for example, are each made from two kinds of atoms.

## Discovering atoms

It is very difficult to cut objects up into atoms as they are so small. We know that atoms do exist because high-powered microscopes can take pictures of them. But atoms were discovered long before these microscopes were invented, so how did people find out that all things are made of such tiny particles? The reason is that we can explain how many things happen if we assume that atoms exist. For example, salt dissolves in water because water pulls the atoms in the salt apart. These are then in the water, which is why it tastes salty.

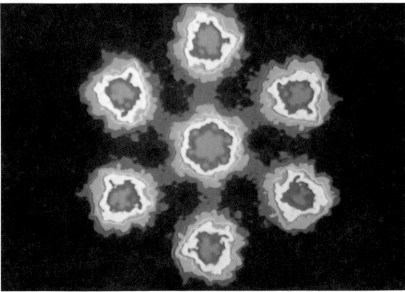

An electron-microscope photograph of uranium atoms

There are 109 elements in all. Russian scientists claimed the discovery of no. 110 in 1988. Everything on Earth is made of one or more of 90 natural elements. Scientists have made 17 new elements, plus numbers 43 and 61, by changing the atoms in existing elements.

Most things are made of different kinds of atoms linked together, but in a few substances, all the atoms are the same. These substances are called elements or chemical elements.

Most elements are solid and many are metals, like iron, gold and silver. Iron contains only iron atoms, gold contains gold atoms, and silver contains silver atoms.

Some elements are gases, like oxygen and nitrogen, the most common gases in air. The atoms of oxygen and nitrogen mix together in air, but they are not linked to each other.

## How atoms differ

All atoms consist of a tiny nucleus at the center surrounded by shells of electrons. Every atom in one particular element normally has the same number of electrons. Atoms have an equal number of electrons and protons — particles inside the nucleus. The number of protons is called the atomic number, and each element has its own.

The atoms below are of three different elements. Carbon has an atomic number of 6 and so has six electrons in each atom. It is usually a soft black solid; soot is made of carbon, for example. Nitro-gen has an atomic number of 7, only one greater than carbon. Yet the extra electron (and proton) in each atom make it totally different, for nitrogen is an invisible gas that is the main gas in air. Silver has an atomic number of 47, and it is a shiny metal.

The electrons move in several shells around the nucleus. Each shell has a maximum number of electrons. The first may contain up to two electrons, the second eight, the third 18, and the fourth shell up to 32 electrons. Atoms can have as many as seven electron shells.

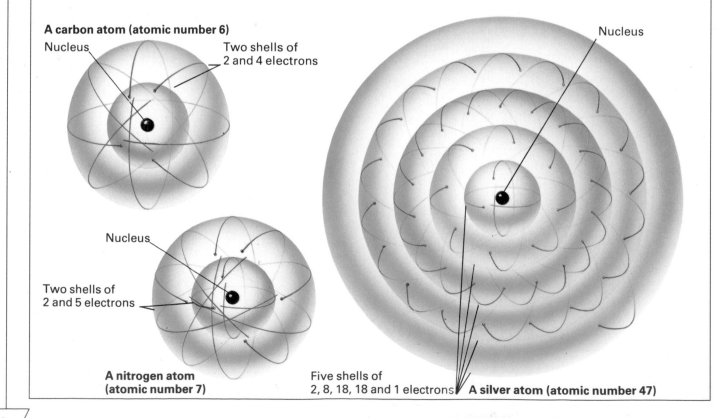

**A carbon atom (atomic number 6)**
Nucleus
Two shells of 2 and 4 electrons

Nucleus
Two shells of 2 and 5 electrons
**A nitrogen atom (atomic number 7)**

Nucleus
Five shells of 2, 8, 18, 18 and 1 electrons
**A silver atom (atomic number 47)**

## Pure elements

We can find some elements in the ground. The shiny yellow metal gold is an element and it occurs in rocks, where it can be found in thin layers or veins, and as little lumps of gold called nuggets. Several other precious metals, including silver and platinum, are also elements that can be dug from the ground. Another important element that is mined is sulfur, a yellow powder used in industry.

Several elements occur as gases. The air is a mixture of oxygen and nitrogen. It also contains other gases, including argon, a gas used in electric lamps, and helium, a light gas used in airships.

A nugget of pure gold

## Useful elements

We make use of several elements in addition to the gold and other precious metals that we fashion into jewelry. The metals iron and aluminum, which are also elements, are used to construct most of the metal objects that we use. One of the most interesting metallic elements is mercury, which is a liquid at normal temperatures. It is used in thermometers, which measure temperature.

Carbon is an unusual element because it can exist in several different forms called allotropes. One is graphite, which is used to make the black lead in a pencil. Another is diamond.

Argon and some other gaseous elements are used in the bright and colorful signs called neon signs. In fact, neon is the name of one of the gases that is used. The signs are made of glass tubes containing the gases, which glow with bright light when an electric current passes through them.

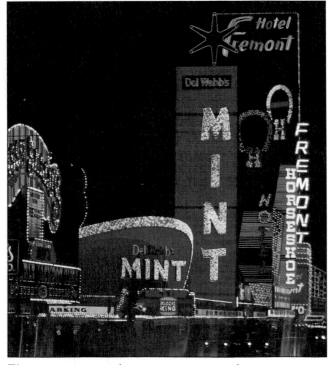
Electric signs use the gases argon and neon

Jewelry made from gold and diamonds

Mercury, in a thermometer, is a liquid metal.

# METALS AND NON-METALS

**The most dense element**: osmium — a metal so heavy that a football made of solid osmium would weigh about the same as three adults.

**The least dense metal**: lithium — so light it can float in water.

**The lightest element**: the gas hydrogen, which is 14 times lighter than air.

There are two main kinds of elements — metals and non-metals. An element belongs to one kind or the other depending on its properties, or characteristics. Metals usually conduct electricity and heat well; this is why electrical wiring and saucepans are made of metal. Except for mercury, they are solid at normal temperature, and pieces of metal are strong yet flexible and can often be bent and shaped without breaking. More than half the elements are metals.

Non-metals are all the other elements, which do not have the same properties as metals.

## The metals we use

One of the most important properties of some metals is that they are very strong. The most common metal is iron. Although it is brittle and can crack easily, we can make it very strong by mixing it with carbon and some other metallic elements. The result is steel, which we use to make all kinds of objects from pins to cars as well as the steel girders and cables that hold up tall buildings and long bridges.

The second most common metal is aluminum, which is light and conducts electricity well. It is therefore used to make aircraft and the long power lines that carry electricity across the country. Aluminum also conducts heat well, so it is used to make saucepans and cooking foil.

Another metal that is of great use is copper, which also conducts electricity well. Electric wires are usually made of copper with a coating of plastic for safety. Copper does not rust or corrode, so it is a good metal for water pipes and tanks. Lead is a heavy metal that bends easily and does not corrode. It is used in sealing roofs on houses.

An electric coil made of copper wire

# Non-metals in use

Many of the non-metallic elements that we use are gases. Hydrogen and helium are the lightest gaseous elements. As they are lighter than air, they are used to fill balloons. Airships once contained hydrogen, but this gas burns in air and it caused several airships to explode. Helium, which is safe, is now used to fill airships. However, hydrogen is a very good fuel and is used in space rockets. Welding torches also burn hydrogen with oxygen gas supplied in cylinders.

Other useful non-metallic elements include chlorine and iodine, which can kill germs. The water in many swimming pools contains chlorine and iodine is a good antiseptic to treat cuts.

One of the most important non-metals is silicon, which is used to make the microchips used in computers. Silicon is a semiconductor — it can be made to change the way it conducts electricity.

An airship is filled with the lighter-than-air gas helium.

Aluminum can be used as thin foil.

Liquid hydrogen is the fuel for the NASA Space Shuttle.

# PUTTING ELEMENTS TOGETHER

The most common compound we use is water, a compound of hydrogen and oxygen.

Although the total number of elements is just over 100, the total number of known compounds is about five million.

The first important alloy was bronze, which was invented about 7,000 years ago. The Bronze Age lasted until about 3,000 years ago, when people discovered how to make iron.

We use only a few elements in their pure form. Often elements are mixed together because the mixture is better than either of the pure elements alone. Mixtures of metals, which are called alloys, are very useful. These include steel (an alloy of iron and carbon plus other metals), brass (copper and zinc) and bronze (copper and tin). Silver-colored coins are made of cupronickel, an alloy of copper and nickel that is very durable.

However, most of the substances that we use are not mixtures but compounds of elements. In compounds, atoms of two or more elements are joined strongly together, usually to form groups of atoms called molecules. Once elements have joined to form compounds, it is difficult to separate them. Most mixtures separate more easily.

## Mixtures and compounds

The beach scene below shows several mixtures and compounds of the elements. The air is a mixture of oxygen, nitrogen, argon and other gases, for example, while the water in the sea is a compound of hydrogen and oxygen. The sea contains salt, which is a compound of chlorine and a metal called sodium, and the sand on the beach is a compound of silicon and oxygen.

The ancient statue is made of bronze. Its green surface is a compound of copper and oxygen which formed when the copper in the bronze reacted with the oxygen in the air.

Many compounds form from a metal and a non-metal, such as salt from sodium and chlorine or the bronze coating from copper and oxygen. Some non-metals pair up to form compounds. Hydrogen and oxygen form water, and form many other compounds with other non-metals.

Sand, water and salt are chemical compounds.

A statue made of bronze, an alloy of copper and tin

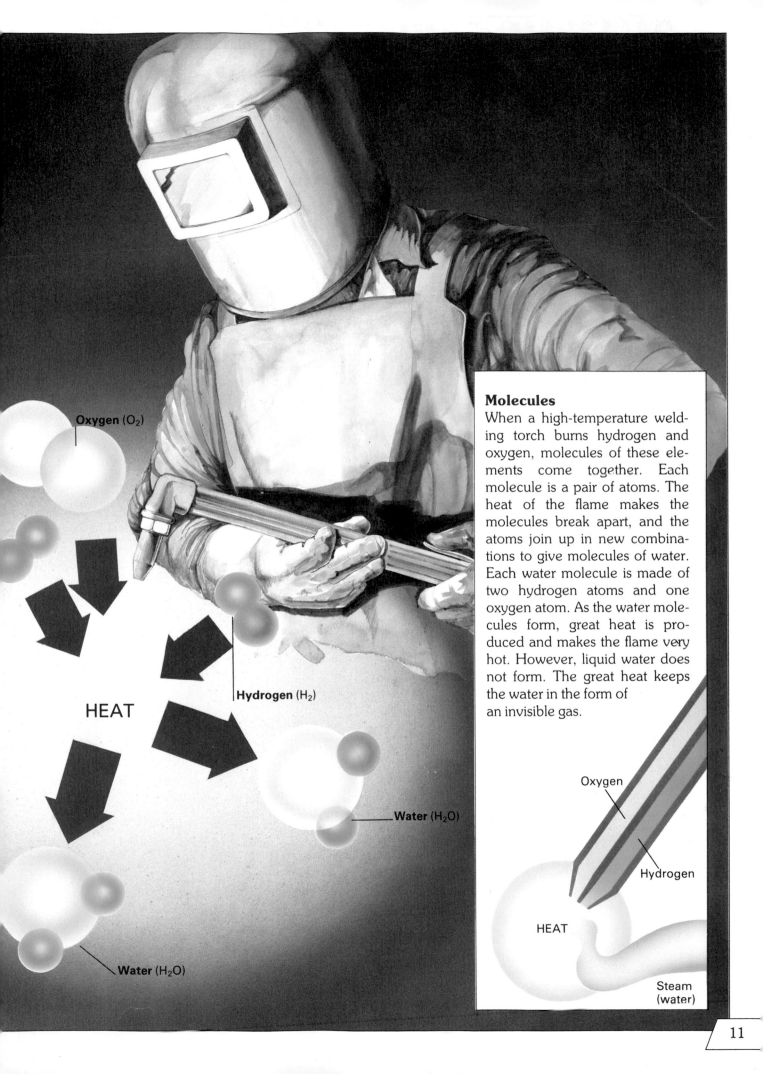

Oxygen (O₂)

HEAT

Hydrogen (H₂)

Water (H₂O)

Water (H₂O)

## Molecules

When a high-temperature welding torch burns hydrogen and oxygen, molecules of these elements come together. Each molecule is a pair of atoms. The heat of the flame makes the molecules break apart, and the atoms join up in new combinations to give molecules of water. Each water molecule is made of two hydrogen atoms and one oxygen atom. As the water molecules form, great heat is produced and makes the flame very hot. However, liquid water does not form. The great heat keeps the water in the form of an invisible gas.

Oxygen

Hydrogen

HEAT

Steam (water)

# CHANGING COMPOUNDS

Most of our energy supplies come from heat produced by burning fuels such as oil, gas and coal.

The noble gases are elements that form very few compounds with other elements. Helium does not burn because it is a noble gas.

Chemistry is the name of the science that deals with elements and compounds. Chemists find out how to make compounds from elements or other compounds, and how to get elements from compounds. Changing compounds in this way is called a chemical reaction. Sometimes the chemical reactions produce heat.

Chemical reactions also include many other important processes, for example, cooking and photography. Chemists can employ chemical reactions to discover new kinds of useful substances, such as plastics, dyes, fertilizers and drugs.

## Making heat

We often burn fuel for heat. Natural gas, which comes from deposits of gas under the ground and beneath the seabed, is a very good fuel. It consists mostly of a compound called methane, which has molecules made of one carbon atom attached to four hydrogen atoms. When methane burns, two oxygen molecules in the air attack each methane molecule. The molecules break apart and all the atoms combine to form different molecules. A molecule of carbon dioxide (which has one carbon atom attached to two oxygen atoms) is produced, plus two molecules of water (one oxygen with two hydrogen) in gaseous form.

As the atoms change partners, heat is produced. An explosion is a reaction that makes heat in the same way but produces it very quickly.

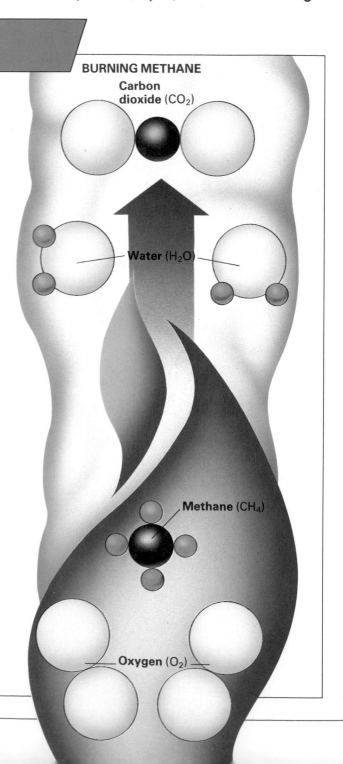

**BURNING METHANE**

Carbon dioxide ($CO_2$)

Water ($H_2O$)

Methane ($CH_4$)

Oxygen ($O_2$)

Natural gas burns in air to produce new chemicals.

# Cooking

Many chemical reactions need heat to work. Cooking is one of them. As the food cooks, the heat causes chemical reactions in which the compounds in the ingredients change.

Too much heat makes food begin to burn, though toasting does this deliberately. Bread and other kinds of food are made of compounds containing carbon, hydrogen and oxygen. When burning starts, the great heat causes the hydrogen and oxygen to form water. This leaves black carbon, which is the charred surface of the toast or burned food.

When burning starts, the reaction begins to use oxygen in the air and produces heat instead of using heat. The toast catches fire, just like the burning trees in a forest fire. The heat then causes more burning. As long as the flames have oxygen from the air, the chemical reaction continues.

Cooking alters meat chemically so that we can eat it.

Burning is a chemical reaction called combustion.

# Rusting

Objects made of iron and steel often get rusty after a long time. Rusting is a very slow chemical reaction that eats away the metal. The iron atoms react with oxygen molecules in the air to form a compound called iron oxide, which is red-brown. This compound is the rust.

Rusting needs water, because rust also contains molecules of water. This is why objects do not rust quickly in dry places.

We can stop rusting by painting the surface of the metal. The layer of paint prevents oxygen and water from getting to the iron so that rusting does not start.

Rusting is an example of an oxidation reaction.

# Smelting

We get metals such as iron from the ground but, unlike gold, most metals do not occur as elements. Instead they occur in rocks as minerals, which are metal compounds. To produce the metals, we smelt the minerals. Smelting makes the metal compound in the mineral change into the metal.

Iron is the most common metal that we use, and we get it from minerals known as iron ore. The ore is a compound of iron, oxygen and silicon, and smelting removes the oxygen and silicon, leaving iron. This is done in a blast furnace, which is a tall tower. Iron ore mixed with coke and limestone is fed into the top of the blast furnace. Hot air from a stove is blasted into the base of the tower.

As the hot air rises through the blast furnace, the oxygen combines with carbon in the coke. This gives great heat, which causes the iron ore to react with the carbon, too. The carbon takes oxygen from the ore, leaving iron. The limestone removes impurities. Molten iron collects at the base of the furnace and is then made into steel in a converter.

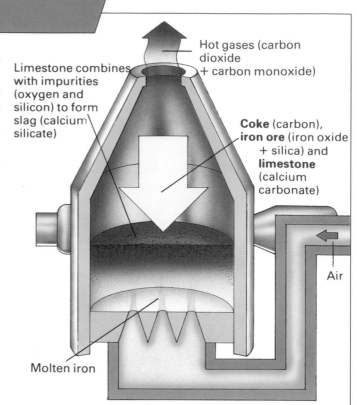

Hot gases (carbon dioxide + carbon monoxide)

Limestone combines with impurities (oxygen and silicon) to form slag (calcium silicate)

**Coke** (carbon), **iron ore** (iron oxide + silica) and **limestone** (calcium carbonate)

Air

Molten iron

Smelting involves complex chemistry to release iron from iron ore.

# Photography

Photography makes use of chemical reactions with silver because some silver compounds change with light. The dark parts of a black-and-white photograph are made of silver, which looks black rather than shiny.

A black-and-white film contains a layer of silver salts, which are compounds of silver with chlorine or bromine. When a camera takes a picture, an image falls on the film for a fraction of a second. The light in the bright parts of the image affects tiny crystals of silver salts in the film. It causes the crystals to begin to break down into silver. Crystals in the dark parts of the image do not break down.

When the film is developed, the reaction proceeds further, so that all the silver salts in the bright parts of the image become dark silver. The remaining silver salts in the dark parts are then dissolved by a fixer. This gives a negative, in which bright parts of the image are dark and dark parts clear.

A print is made by forming an image of the negative on to photographic paper, which has a coating of silver salts like the film. When the print is developed and fixed, the bright and dark parts of the negative reverse.

Color photography works in basically the same way except that when film and prints are developed, the silver is changed to layers of colored dyes.

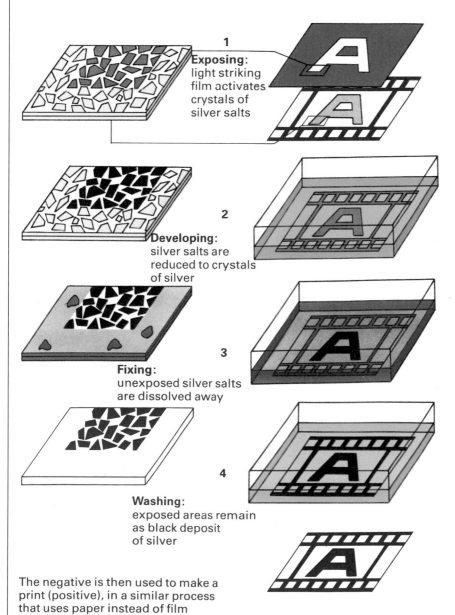

**1 Exposing:** light striking film activates crystals of silver salts

**2 Developing:** silver salts are reduced to crystals of silver

**3 Fixing:** unexposed silver salts are dissolved away

**4 Washing:** exposed areas remain as black deposit of silver

The negative is then used to make a print (positive), in a similar process that uses paper instead of film

∧ photographic negative

# SOLUTIONS

Seawater is a solution of salt in water. Each liter contains about 28 grams of salt plus another 8 grams of other compounds.

Hard water is called "hard" because it is a solution of mineral compounds. Soft water contains few minerals.

When chemical reactions happen, the molecules of the elements and compounds must first meet and then react. This readily occurs with liquids or gases because their molecules can move and mix together. This does not happen as easily with solids so they do not react easily with each other.

Many reactions therefore take place in solutions. A solid is first dissolved in a liquid, often water. The liquid molecules force the molecules of the solid compound apart so that they are free to move. They then react with other molecules that are present in, or enter, the solution.

## Columns in caves

Slender white columns called stalactites hang from the roofs of many caves, while stalagmites rise from the floor. The columns are made of a compound called calcium carbonate. They form very slowly as rain water trickles down through limestone rock above the cave. The water dissolves calcium carbonate in the limestone. When the water reaches the cave, it drips from the roof to the floor. The calcium carbonate leaves the solution and builds up the columns.

Calcium carbonate forms columns in caves.

## Fizzy drinks

Drinks are solutions in water of compounds that give taste and color to the drinks. Fizzy drinks also contain the gas carbon dioxide, which is dissolved in the water. It gives a sharp taste and also makes the drink fizz. When the drink is poured out, the carbon dioxide begins to leave the solution. It forms bubbles of gas that rise through the drink and make it fizz. Powders that make fizzy drinks react to produce carbon dioxide as they dissolve in water.

Carbon dioxide bubbles from a dissolving tablet

## Making crystals

If a solution of a solid substance is left, some of the water evaporates. Water molecules leave the solution and enter the air. Soon, the solution has more molecules of the substance than it can hold and the substance begins to leave the solution. The molecules of the substance begin to attach themselves to the container. More and more solid molecules build up there, and crystals of the substance begin to form. They grow as more water is lost until all the water has gone, leaving a layer of crystals on the container. Salt is obtained from sea water in this way. The sea water flows into pools called salt pans by the shore, and the water then evaporates, leaving salt crystals.

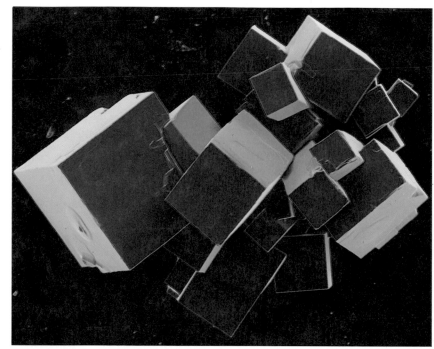

Close-up of crystals of common salt (sodium chloride)

## Acid attack

Some solutions can dissolve many different substances. Acids are among these solutions, and strong acids can even dissolve metals like steel.

Acids dissolve in a different way than water. The acid molecules react with the atoms or molecules in the metal or rock, forming compounds that then dissolve in the solution.

Acid rain contains acid that comes from burning fuel. Fumes enter the air from the chimneys of power stations, factories and homes and also the exhausts of cars and trucks. Some of the fumes dissolve in the rain drops, making the rain acid. When the rain falls, the acid in it begins to destroy trees and other plants, life in lakes and ponds, and the stone in buildings.

Acid fog and rain kill thousands of fir trees.

# ELECTRICITY AND ATOMS

When a flashlight is lit, about 20 quintillion electrons pass through the wire in the bulb every second.

The 1st scientist to produce an electric current used a dead frog and two pieces of different metals. The battery was developed from this discovery in 1800.

When electricity flows along a wire or enters anything, tiny particles called electrons move. These are the same electrons that make up atoms. We can make electricity by getting the electrons to leave some atoms and move along a wire. This happens when we use a battery.

The process known as electrolysis uses electricity to get elements from compounds by adding electrons to their atoms or by taking electrons away. Gases such as chlorine and several metals are produced in this way. This is also the basis of electroplating.

## Batteries

Inside a battery are two electrodes and a solution or paste called an electrolyte. The battery terminals are connected to the electrodes. When the battery is used, the elements and compounds in the electrodes and the electrolyte react together and change to new compounds. Electrons then move from atoms in one electrode to the other.

The electric current continues to flow until all the elements and compounds have changed. Then the battery is dead. Some batteries, like those in cars, can be recharged with an electric current. This reverses the reaction and produces the original substances in the electrodes and electrolyte.

Electrodes of a silver-zinc battery and their case

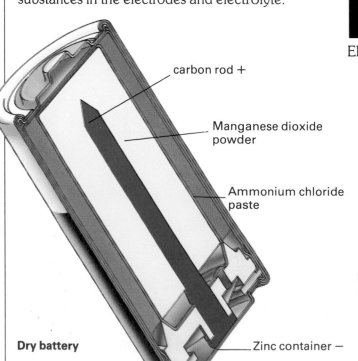

carbon rod +

Manganese dioxide powder

Ammonium chloride paste

**Dry battery**

Zinc container −

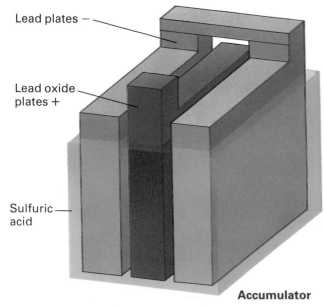

Lead plates −

Lead oxide plates +

Sulfuric acid

**Accumulator**

# Electrical extraction

Aluminum and several other metals cannot be easily obtained by smelting their ores. Instead, we use a process called electrolysis. In this process, a strong electric current is passed through a container of molten ore. The atoms in the ore move apart, and the metal atoms lose electrons and gain a positive electric charge. They are then attracted to the electrode with a negative electric charge (a cathode), because unlike electric charges attract. There they form molten metal. The other atoms in the ore go to the other electrode, which has a positive electric charge (an anode).

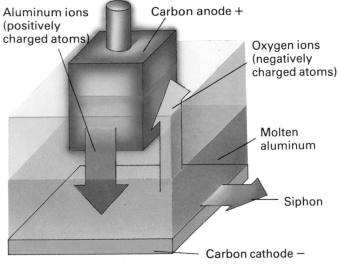

Aluminum ions (positively charged atoms)

Carbon anode +

Oxygen ions (negatively charged atoms)

Molten aluminum

Siphon

Carbon cathode −

Aluminum is extracted using electricity.

# Electroplating

Many objects have a tough and attractive coating of metals such as gold, silver, copper, nickel or chromium. Electroplating is the process that deposits a thin layer of metal over all the surface. The object is dipped in a solution of a compound of the metal. In the solution, the metal atoms in the compound have an electric charge — they are ions. The solution also contains a rod, often of the same metal. When electricity is passed through the rod, solution and object, metal ions (electrically charged atoms) move to the object's surface, building up a layer of metal.

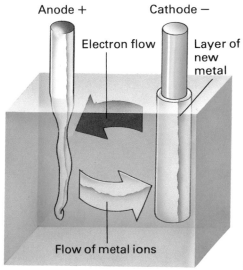

Anode +

Cathode −

Electron flow

Layer of new metal

Flow of metal ions

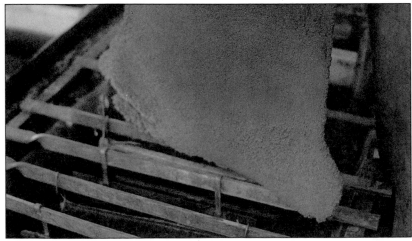

Copper electroplating

# CRYSTALS

The largest crystal is a huge piece of the mineral beryl as big as a house. It weighs 400 tons.

Tiny crystals of the mineral quartz enable clocks and watches to keep very good time. They make regular electric signals which control the hands or time-display.

Several elements and many compounds form crystals. They include carbon in diamond, and such common substances as salt, sugar and ice. A crystal is a piece of a pure element or compound that forms in the same shape. Salt crystals are tiny cubes, for example, and ice crystals are like small six-pointed stars. Crystals have particular shapes because the atoms of the elements inside join together in certain patterns. The ways in which the atoms join give crystals many special uses. The microchips in computers, for example, are made from crystals.

## Inside crystals

The atoms of the elements in a crystal link together in a pattern called a lattice. Crystals can grow as extra atoms join on to the lattice. The extra atoms extend the lattice to keep the same pattern throughout the crystal. The shape and properties of the crystal depend on its lattice. A salt crystal, for example, contains sodium atoms and chlorine atoms. The atoms link in straight rows to give a cubic pattern, and the crystals are cubic in shape. Diamond contains atoms of carbon linked together so that each atom bonds to four other atoms. The bonds are very strong, and the pattern in which the atoms grip one another makes diamond very hard.

The bonds between atoms in crystals and in molecules form in two main ways. Ionic bonds form when one or more electrons transfer from one atom to another. The transfer gives the atoms different electric charges, and they are pulled together. Sodium and chlorine in salt have ionic bonds. Covalent bonds form when the outer electrons move between two or more atoms so that they share the electrons between them. The sharing pulls the atoms together. Carbon atoms in diamond join together with covalent bonds.

Salt crystal structure

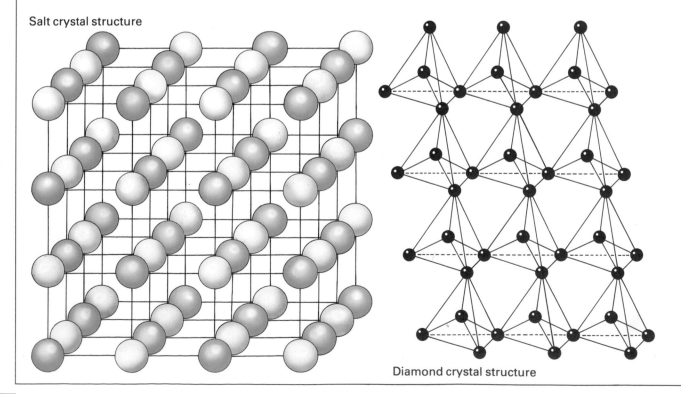

Diamond crystal structure

## Natural crystals

Crystals of all kinds are common in nature. Many minerals formed as crystals when solutions of the minerals evaporated or molten minerals cooled and became solid. Some of the crystals look very attractive, and we use them for ornaments and jewelry. Gemstones, such as diamonds and rubies, are also natural crystals but their faces are cut so that they glitter with light.

Water forms small ice crystals when it freezes making snow and frost. A snowflake is a mass of ice crystals. The water molecules link together in the crystal in a six-sided pattern that makes the crystals grow like stars. This can be seen with a microscope.

Ice crystals resemble feathery stars.

## Growing crystals

It is possible to grow crystals. Suspend a tiny crystal on the end of a thread in a strong solution of the substance; sugar is a good choice. As the solution slowly evaporates, atoms in the solution join the crystal and it may slowly grow in size. Crystals may also grow on the sides of the container.

To make microchips, computer manufacturers first grow large crystals of silicon from molten silicon. Then they slice the crystal into thin disks from which many microchips are made. Silicon atoms link up in a similar way to the carbon atoms in diamond. However, the manufacturers put in small amounts of other atoms, which link up to the silicon atoms in the same pattern. This affects the way that electric currents pass through the silicon, so the microchip can handle electric signals.

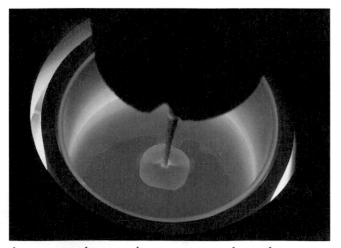

A pure simple crystal growing in molten silicon

Silicon crystals are made into electronic microchips.

# CARBON COMPOUNDS

There are about 4.5 million carbon compounds, nine times as many compounds as the compounds of all the other elements put together.

Molecules of the carbon compounds called nucleic acids, such as DNA, contain millions of atoms linked together.

Carbon is one of the most common elements. It makes up diamond, graphite, coke and soot, and its compounds include the gas carbon dioxide and calcium carbonate, the compound in limestone and also chalk. However, there are many, many more carbon compounds, and they are very important. The chemistry of carbon and its compounds is called organic chemistry. This is because it was once thought that these compounds were produced only by living things. The other elements and their compounds make up inorganic chemistry, as it was thought that they occur only in non-living things such as minerals. We now know that both kinds of compounds occur in living and non-living things, but the names have stuck.

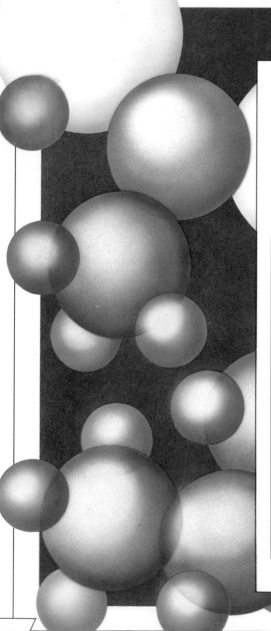

Carbon is a key element because it is the basis of all life on Earth. This results from the unique ability of carbon atoms to join to each other to make giant molecules, including the proteins, fats and carbohydrates in animal tissues and the compounds such as starch and cellulose that make up the main structures of plants. Some smaller carbon compounds are shown on the right.

Animals and plants contain carbon compounds.

# A key element

Carbon compounds are very important because they are the main compounds present in our bodies and other living things. Compounds such as fats, proteins, starch and sugars, which make up our food, are carbon compounds and so too are vitamins and drugs. Natural fibers such as silk, wool and cotton, which come from animals and plants, are also carbon compounds.

Other important materials and substances are made of carbon compounds. They include paper, rubber, dyes, soap, detergents, fuels such as wood, coal, gasoline, oil and natural gas, and also all the many kinds of plastics and artificial fibers.

All common dyes are compounds of carbon.

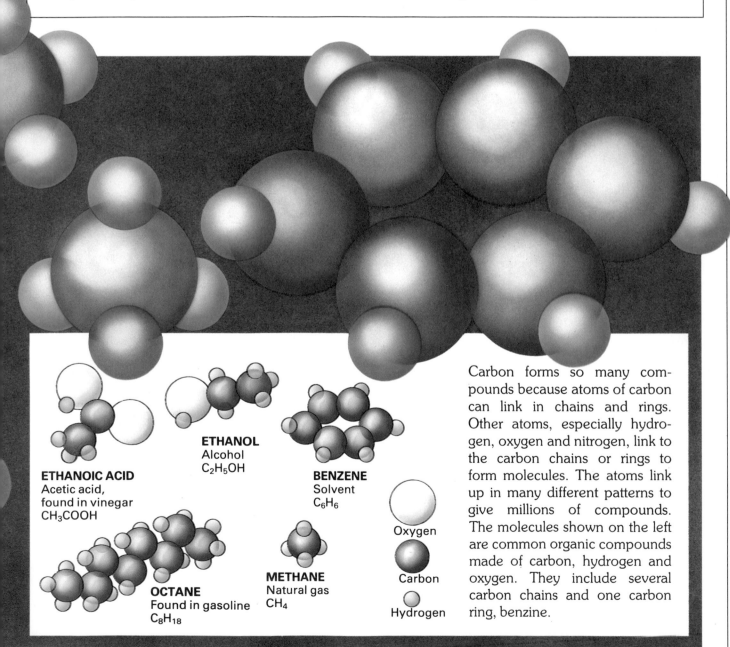

**ETHANOIC ACID**
Acetic acid,
found in vinegar
$CH_3COOH$

**ETHANOL**
Alcohol
$C_2H_5OH$

**BENZENE**
Solvent
$C_6H_6$

**OCTANE**
Found in gasoline
$C_8H_{18}$

**METHANE**
Natural gas
$CH_4$

Oxygen

Carbon

Hydrogen

Carbon forms so many compounds because atoms of carbon can link in chains and rings. Other atoms, especially hydrogen, oxygen and nitrogen, link to the carbon chains or rings to form molecules. The atoms link up in many different patterns to give millions of compounds. The molecules shown on the left are common organic compounds made of carbon, hydrogen and oxygen. They include several carbon chains and one carbon ring, benzine.

# GIANT MOLECULES

The first polymer to be made was a plastic called Bakelite. It was invented in 1909 and was the foundation for the plastics industry. The latest plastics are so tough that they are stronger than steel and do not burn. These plastics are beginning to replace metal.

The carbon chains in the molecules of carbon compounds can be extremely long. Many compounds with giant molecules are called polymers. All the plastics that we use are polymers, which is why several have names beginning with "poly," such as polyethylene and polyester.

Natural polymers occur in plants, but most of the polymers that we use are made in factories. They are made from simple carbon compounds with small molecules, many of which come from the oil that we get from under the ground and seabed.

## Making polymers

Polymers are made by a process called polymerization. This starts with compounds that have short chains of carbon atoms, often with just two atoms. These compounds are called monomers. The plastic polyethylene, often known as polythene, is made from the monomer ethylene (ethene). This is a gas in which the molecules each have a chain of two carbon atoms. Two hydrogen atoms are attached to each carbon atom in the chain. To make polymerization take place, the gas is heated and compressed. Substances called catalysts help polymerization to occur, and the short chains of the ethylene molecules attach themselves to each other end to end and form very long chains of carbon atoms. Pairs of hydrogen atoms remain attached to each carbon atom in the chain. The long carbon chains make polyethylene a flexible solid.

Other polymers are made from monomers in the same kind of way. Polystyrene is made by polymerizing styrene, for example. Some polymers, often called copolymers, are made from two monomers.

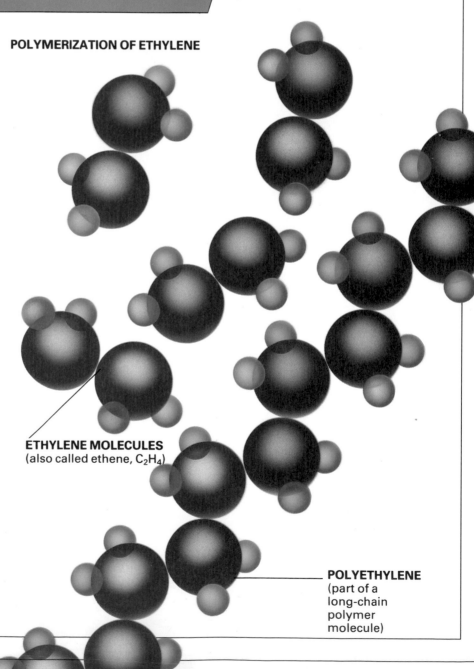

**POLYMERIZATION OF ETHYLENE**

**ETHYLENE MOLECULES**
(also called ethene, $C_2H_4$)

**POLYETHYLENE**
(part of a long-chain polymer molecule)

# Natural polymers

Plants contain several natural polymers, including starch, which we eat in potatoes, wheat and rice. Cellulose is another natural polymer found in the stems and roots of plants; cotton is made of cellulose. The molecules of starch and cellulose contain thousands of carbon rings linked together.

Another natural polymer is rubber. The long-chain molecules in natural rubber bend easily, which makes it too soft for use. In vulcanization, a process to make rubber harder, it is heated with sulfur, and the sulfur atoms link the chains together to make the rubber harder yet still flexible.

Tapping a tree for rubber – a natural polymer

# Plastics

Before plastics were invented, people used mainly natural materials to make things. These materials included wood, metals, ceramics and natural fibers such as wool and cotton to make cloth. During the last 120 years, chemists have discovered how to make many artificial materials. The first of these materials made use of cellulose extracted from plants. The fabric rayon is made of cellulose fibers.

The discovery of polymerization has enabled chemists to make many new kinds of materials that do not exist in nature. These materials are called polymers or plastics. They can be made with many different properties for all kinds of uses, and we now often use plastics and fibers made from plastics instead of natural materials. Plastics can be cheaper and it is often easier to make objects of plastics than to use natural materials. Polymerization has also given us high-quality long-lasting paints and very strong adhesives.

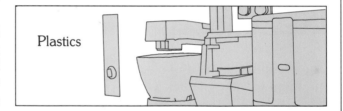
Plastics

A modern home has dozens of objects made from plastics.

## Soft and flexible plastics

Many plastics are useful because they are soft or flexible. They include polyethylene, PVC (polyvinyl chloride), nylon, polyesters, polystyrene and polycarbonate plastics. They are often used to make flexible containers, such as bowls, pipes, wrappings and plastic foams. All these plastics are known as thermoplastics because they soften when they are heated and harden when they cool. This makes it easy to mold thermoplastics into objects. They are polymers in which the long chains of carbon atoms are mostly separate from each other. Heat makes thermoplastics soft or flexible. However, several of them, such as nylon, are strong and hard when they are cooled.

Thermoplastics are used in toys.

## Hard and rigid plastics

The second main kind of plastics are thermosetting plastics, which are hard and rigid. The first plastic, Bakelite, was a thermosetting plastic. The polymer hardens as it sets. Unlike thermoplastics, thermosetting plastics do not soften when heated later.

Thermosetting plastics are no longer used for many objects as they tend to be brittle and may break. But they are very useful as resins for adhesives, varnishes and paints because they set to give a very strong bond to surfaces. Unlike thermoplastics, the long carbon chains in the molecules link to each other as the polymer forms. The links between the chains prevent the chains from bending and make the polymer hard and rigid.

Strong glues are made from thermosetting plastics.

# Artificial fibers

Fibers can be made of plastics such as nylon or polyester or the natural polymer cellulose. These fibers are strong, and can be made into fabrics for clothes which are crease-resistant. Other uses include carpets, which are often made with a plastic backing, and toothbrushes with nylon bristles set in a plastic handle.

Artificial fibers are made from a solution of the plastic or from molten plastic. Rayon, which is cellulose, is made from a solution of cellulose prepared from wood. The solution or molten plastic is forced through a "spinneret" containing fine holes, often into another solution, so that the plastic or polymer solidifies. Long fibers emerge from the holes, and are made into yarn.

New materials that are light but extremely strong make use of carbon fibers. These are prepared by heating plastic fibers to form threads of pure carbon. These carbon fibers are then embedded in a plastic resin, which sets to give a material that is reinforced by the fibers inside. Carbon-reinforced plastics are used to make tennis rackets and components for aircraft, in which strength and lightness are important qualities.

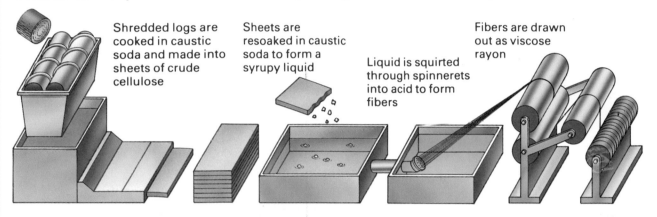

Shredded logs are cooked in caustic soda and made into sheets of crude cellulose

Sheets are resoaked in caustic soda to form a syrupy liquid

Liquid is squirted through spinnerets into acid to form fibers

Fibers are drawn out as viscose rayon

Artificial fibers are used to weave fabrics and carpets.

The simplest nucleus is that of the hydrogen atom. It contains just one proton. Among natural elements, the biggest nucleus is that of the uranium atom. It contains 92 protons and 146 neutrons packed together.

A quadrillion protons or neutrons would together weigh just over a gram. Electrons are almost 2,000 times lighter than protons and neutrons.

The tiny nucleus at the center of every atom is made up of particles called protons and neutrons. Each proton has a positive electric charge, while each electron moving around the nucleus has a negative electric charge. A neutron has no electric charge. Because an atom normally has the same number of protons and electrons, the positive and negative charges balance each other so overall the atom has no electric charge.

Atoms may lose or gain electrons. If an atom gains electrons, it has more negative charges than positive charges from the protons in the nucleus and so has an overall negative charge. An atom that loses electrons will have more protons than electrons and so has an overall positive electric charge. Charged atoms are called ions.

## Weighing atoms

Atoms have so little mass that we cannot put them on a balance to weigh them. Instead, scientists use a mass spectrograph to do this. This machine produces a beam of moving ions by giving the atoms electric charges. Some ions pass through the slit to give a narrow beam. The beam then passes through two more charged plates and between the poles of a magnet. This makes the beam curve so that the atoms strike a detector, such as a photographic plate. The lighter atoms curve more than the heavier atoms, and the beam spreads out into bands of atoms with different masses as it strikes the detector. From the position of each band, scientists can measure the mass of the atoms in it. The mass spectrograph also measures the number of atoms in each band.

Because the electrons in an atom are so much lighter than the nucleus, the mass spectrograph effectively measures the mass of the nucleus of each atom. From this, the number of protons and neutrons can be found.

The mass spectrograph can also identify the atoms in a substance. A space probe now flying to the moons of Mars carries one to find which elements are in the surface of the moons.

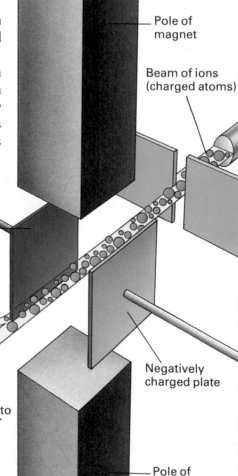

Pole of magnet

Beam of ions (charged atoms)

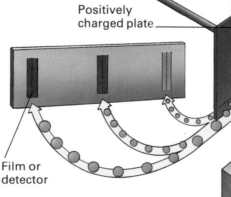

Positively charged plate

Negatively charged plate

Film or detector

Ions are sorted according to weight, with heavier ones going the farthest

Pole of magnet

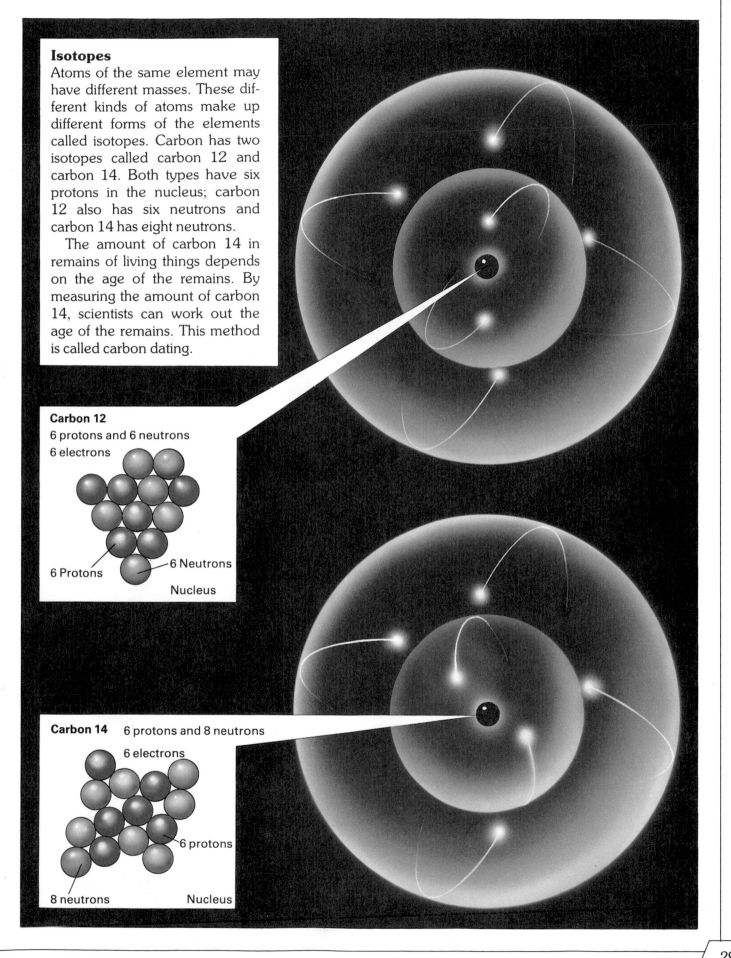

## Isotopes

Atoms of the same element may have different masses. These different kinds of atoms make up different forms of the elements called isotopes. Carbon has two isotopes called carbon 12 and carbon 14. Both types have six protons in the nucleus; carbon 12 also has six neutrons and carbon 14 has eight neutrons.

The amount of carbon 14 in remains of living things depends on the age of the remains. By measuring the amount of carbon 14, scientists can work out the age of the remains. This method is called carbon dating.

**Carbon 12**
6 protons and 6 neutrons
6 electrons

6 Protons

6 Neutrons

Nucleus

**Carbon 14**   6 protons and 8 neutrons
6 electrons

6 protons

8 neutrons          Nucleus

# RADIOACTIVITY

Radioactivity was discovered by accident in 1896 when radiation from a uranium compound made a photographic plate go dark.

Radioactive isotopes lose their radioactivity. Some do so in a fraction of a second, while others remain radioactive for billions of years.

Some isotopes are radioactive — they give off, or are capable of giving off, radiation. In this process, energy in the form of rays of light or heat, is sent out of atoms that have unstable nuclei. This instability occurs when there are either too many or too few neutrons in the nucleus. To correct this, the nucleus produces bursts of radiation. This radiation can be harmful to living things, and some people who work with highly radioactive substances have to be shielded from their radiation. But radioactivity also has uses that are helpful rather than harmful.

## Three kinds of radiation

Radioactive isotopes emit three kinds of radiation: alpha particles, beta particles and gamma rays, although no one atom emits all three kinds at once. An alpha particle contains two protons and two neutrons. These particles are not very penetrating, and are stopped by a sheet of paper. Beta particles are electrons emitted from atoms. They are a hundred times as penetrating as alpha particles, but a sheet of aluminum 3 mm thick will stop them.

Gamma rays are the third kind of radiation. They are not particles, but invisible rays similar to X rays. Gamma rays are very penetrating, and need a thick sheet of lead or concrete to stop them.

Radioactivity causes one element to change into another. Emitting an alpha particle or beta particle causes the make-up of the nucleus to change, and it becomes the nucleus of a different element.

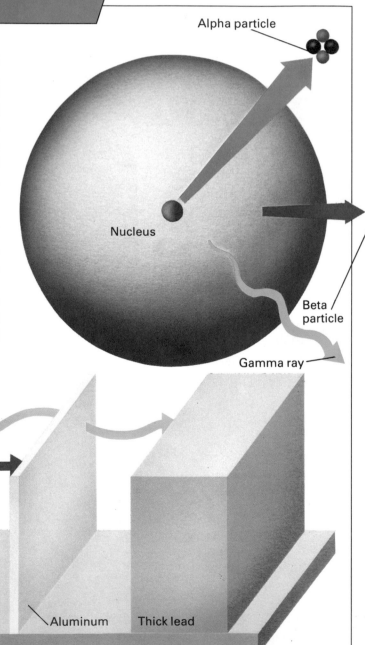

Alpha particle

Nucleus

Beta particle

Gamma ray

**ABSORPTION OF PARTICLES**

Gamma rays

Beta particle

Alpha particles

Paper          Aluminum     Thick lead

## Sources of radioactivity

Several radioactive isotopes occur in minerals in the ground. These include the elements uranium, thorium and radium. Another radioactive element in the earth is the gas radon. We can also make radioactive isotopes by bombarding elements with protons, neutrons or alpha particles. The nuclei absorb the particles and change into nuclei of radioactive isotopes.

"Yellow cake" stage in uranium ore extraction

## Detecting radioactivity

Several instruments can detect radiation, which is useful for checking for radioactivity and for discovering radioactive minerals. Photographic film is affected by rays and particles, and turns dark as if it had been exposed to light. A geiger counter can count the number of particles, while bubble chambers and cloud chambers show up tracks made by particles or rays passing through.

A geiger counter measures radioactivity.

## Using radioactivity

Radiation is harmful to living things because the particles and rays affect the atoms in living cells. They change the number of electrons and may alter the nucleus. The affected atoms can cause changes in the cells that bring disease. However, radioactivity can help people with cancer, who have some cells that are not normal. Giving cancer patients doses of radiation can kill the harmful cancer cells.

Radioactivity also has uses in industry. Gamma rays from a strongly radioactive isotope can pass through pipes and other metal parts in machines. A detector picks up the rays and shows up any cracks and flaws inside the metal that could cause the parts to fail.

Another important use is in tracers. These are slightly radioactive solutions which are given to plants and animals. A detector can then follow the movement of the tracer through the plant or animal. This helps scientists to find out about the living processes inside plants and animals.

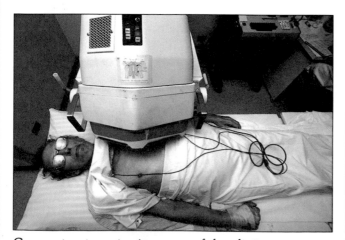

Cancer treatment using powerful radiation

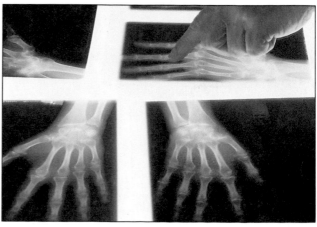

X-ray photographs are helpful to doctors.

Nuclear energy was first released in a nuclear reactor built in 1942.

The reactors in nuclear power stations and nuclear submarines produce waste that remains radioactive for thousands of years.

Strong forces hold the protons and neutrons together inside the nucleus of every atom. Nuclear energy is released when the nuclei of atoms in the nuclear fuel split. This releases huge amounts of energy from the nuclear fuel. For example, a kilogram of uranium can produce two million times as much energy as a kilogram of coal. In nuclear power stations, this energy is used to generate electricity, which goes to homes, offices, schools and factories. Nuclear weapons also release nuclear energy in a huge explosion that can be powerful enough to destroy whole cities.

## Nuclear fission

Fission is the main way of producing nuclear energy. It uses isotopes of uranium or plutonium for fuel. Free neutrons moving about in the fuel start fission. When a neutron strikes the nucleus of an atom of fuel, it can cause the nucleus to break into two smaller nuclei. This is nuclear fission. The nucleus also emits more neutrons as it splits. These neutrons can then cause more fission in other nuclei, which produce more neutrons and so on. The free neutrons and the split nuclei move at very high speed, which is converted to very great heat. This heat is the nuclear energy, and large amounts of heat come from small amounts of nuclear fuel.

This process, in which fission occurs in one nucleus after another, is called a chain reaction. In a nuclear weapon, the chain reaction proceeds very quickly so that the sudden release of great heat produces an explosion. In the nuclear reactor of a nuclear power station, the chain reaction proceeds slowly. Nuclear fission produces dangerously large amounts of radiation and also radioactive waste.

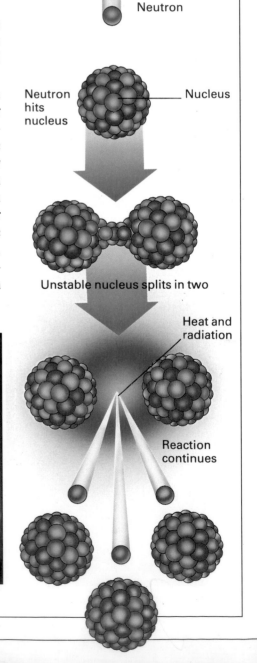

Neutron

Neutron hits nucleus — Nucleus

Unstable nucleus splits in two

Heat and radiation

Reaction continues

A nuclear explosion releases huge amounts of radio active fall-out.

# Nuclear reactors

Nuclear power stations and nuclear submarines contain nuclear reactors. In a reactor are rods containing uranium or other fissionable fuel, a moderator and control rods. The moderator slows down the neutrons to help fission occur in the fuel rods. The control rods absorb neutrons to slow down or stop the chain reaction. A coolant flows through the reactor and carries away the heat produced. The hot coolant then flows to a heat exchanger, where it causes water to boil. The steam produced then goes to power a steam turbine.

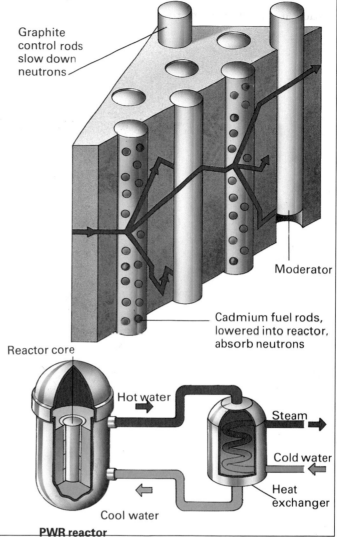

Graphite control rods slow down neutrons

Moderator

Cadmium fuel rods, lowered into reactor, absorb neutrons

A Soviet icebreaker with nuclear-powered engines

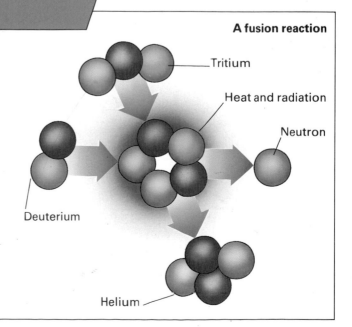

Reactor core

Hot water

Steam

Cold water

Heat exchanger

Cool water

**PWR reactor**

# Nuclear fusion

Fusion is another method of releasing nuclear energy. It uses very light elements, which have to be heated to a temperature of millions of degrees. This forces the atoms together so strongly that the protons and neutrons in their nuclei combine to form larger nuclei. This process produces large amounts of energy. Deuterium and tritium, which are isotopes of hydrogen, can fuse to form the element helium and release free neutrons. This happens in powerful nuclear weapons. A fission explosion first produces the very high temperature, which sets off a fusion explosion.

Scientists are also trying to produce controlled nuclear fusion in special reactors that create the high temperature required.

**A fusion reaction**

Tritium

Heat and radiation

Neutron

Deuterium

Helium

33

# THE PERIODIC TABLE

Scientists use a special table of the elements called the Periodic Table. Each element has a chemical symbol as well as its name and atomic number. The elements are organized according to the arrangement of electrons within their electron shells. This puts elements with similar properties into the same column. The main groups are the numbered columns in the table. Group 1 contains the alkali metals, which are highly reactive, while group 7 contains the highly reactive non-metals called the halogens. Group 8 contains the unreactive noble gases.

Between groups 2 and 3 are sets of elements known as the transition elements. These elements are similar to their horizontal neighbors as well as to their vertical neighbors. The lanthanides (58-71) and the actinides (90-103) make up two horizontal sets of similar elements. All the elements above uranium (element 92) are artificial. There are several elements above element 103, which is the highest element normally shown.

**KEY**

| | |
|---|---|
| HYDROGEN | |
| ALKALI AND ALKALINE EARTH METALS | |
| METALS | |
| NON-METALS INCLUDING HALOGENS | |
| NOBLE GASES | |
| LANTHAN-IDES AND ACTINIDES | |

| Group I | II | | | | | | | | | | | | | | Group III | IV | V | VI | VII | VIII |
|---|---|---|---|---|---|---|---|---|---|---|---|---|---|---|---|---|---|---|---|---|
| | | | | | | | | | 1 H hydrogen | | | | | | | | | | | 2 He helium |
| 3 Li lithium | 4 Be beryllium | | | | | | | | | | | | | | 5 B boron | 6 C carbon | 7 N nitrogen | 8 O oxygen | 9 F fluorine | 10 Ne neon |
| 11 Na sodium | 12 Mg magnesium | 1 | | | | | | | | | | | | | 13 Al aluminum | 14 Si silicon | 15 P phosphorus | 16 S sulfur | 17 Cl chlorine | 18 Ar argon |
| 19 K potassium | 20 Ca calcium | 21 Sc scandium | 22 Ti titanium | 23 V vanadium | 24 Cr chromium | 25 Mn manganese | 26 Fe iron | 27 Co cobalt | 28 Ni nickel | 29 Cu copper | 30 Zn zinc | | | | 31 Ga gallium | 32 Ge germanium | 33 As arsenic | 34 Se selenium | 35 Br bromine | 36 Kr krypton |
| 37 Rb rubidium | 38 Sr strontium | 39 Y yttrium | 40 Zr zirconium | 41 Nb niobium | 42 Mo molybdenum | 43 Tc technetium | 44 Ru ruthenium | 45 Rh rhodium | 46 Pd palladium | 47 Ag silver | 48 Cd cadmium | | | | 49 In indium | 50 Sn tin | 51 Sb antimony | 52 Te tellurium | 53 I iodine | 54 Xe xenon |
| 55 Cs cesium | 56 Ba barium | 57 La lanthanum | 72 Hf hafnium | 73 Ta tantalum | 74 W tungsten | 75 Re rhenium | 76 Os osmium | 77 Ir iridium | 78 Pt platinum | 79 Au gold | 80 Hg mercury | | | | 81 Tl thallium | 82 Pb lead | 83 Bi bismuth | 84 Po polonium | 85 At astatine | 86 Rn radon |
| 87 Fr francium | 88 Ra radium | 89 Ac actinium | | | | | | | | | | | | | | | | | | |

| 58 Ce cerium | 59 Pr praseodymium | 60 Nd neodymium | 61 Pm promethium | 62 Sm samarium | 63 Eu europium | 64 Gd gadolinium | 65 Tb terbium | 66 Dy dysprosium | 67 Ho holmium | 68 Er erbium | 69 Tm thulium | 70 Yb ytterbium | 71 Lu lutetium |
|---|---|---|---|---|---|---|---|---|---|---|---|---|---|
| 90 Th thorium | 91 Pa protactinium | 92 U uranium | 93 Np neptunium | 94 Pu plutonium | 95 Am americium | 96 Cm curium | 97 Bk berkelium | 98 Cf californium | 99 Es einsteinium | 100 Fm fermium | 101 Md mendelevium | 102 No nobelium | 103 Lr lawrencium |

# GLOSSARY

**air** Consists of nitrogen, oxygen, argon, carbon dioxide, water vapor and small amounts of other gases.

**allotropes** Forms of an element that have different physical properties.

**alloy** A mixture of two or more metallic elements.

**anode** The positive terminal of an electrolytic cell.

**atomic number** The number of protons in the nucleus of an atom of an element.

**atoms** The tiny particles of which everything is made.

**cathode** The negative terminal of an electrolytic cell.

**chemical reaction** A reaction in which elements or compounds react together so that their atoms combine in different ways.

**compound** A substance in which two or more elements are combined so that their atoms are linked together.

**crystal** A solid substance that always forms in a particular shape.

**electron** A very tiny particle that has a negative electric charge.

**element** A substance that contains the same kind of atoms.

**energy** What is needed for actions to happen; forms of energy include heat, light and electricity.

**gaseous element** An element that is a gas at normal temperatures.

**ion** An atom with an electric charge.

**isotope** A form of an element in which the nuclei of the atoms have the same number of neutrons.

**metal** A substance that is generally shiny, hard, flexible and heavy, and which conducts heat and electricity well.

**metallic element** An element that is a metal.

**mineral** A compound that occurs in the ground and that has certain properties such as hardness and crystalline structure.

**molecule** A group of atoms linked together.

**monomer** Compound that has short chains of carbon atoms.

**neutron** A very tiny particle inside the nucleus of an atom. It has no electric charge.

**noble gases** The elements helium, neon, argon, krypton, xenon and radon. They form very few compounds.

**non-metal** An element that does not have the properties of a metal.

**nucleus (plural nuclei)** The central part of every atom.

**ore** A mineral containing a useful metallic element.

**plastics** Various synethically-produced (usually from organic compounds by polymerization) non-metallic compounds, which can be molded into various forms and hardened for commercial use.

**polymer** A substance that contains very large molecules each composed of small molecules linked together.

**properties** The characteristics of an element. Physical properties are facts such as its color, hardness and density, while its chemical properties are the way the element reacts with other elements.

**proton** A very tiny particle inside the nucleus of an atom. It has a postive electric charge.

**radiation** The streams of particles or rays produced by radioactivity.

**radioactivity** The production of streams of particles or rays by the nuclei of atoms.

**smelting** The extraction of a metal from its ore with the use of heat.

**solution** A liquid in which another substance is dissolved.

**spinneret** A machine with very fine holes through which molten plastic is forced.

**uranium** An element that is used in the production of nuclear energy.

# INDEX

All entries in bold are found in the Glossary

**Photographic Credits:**
l = left, r = right, t = top, b = bottom, m = middle
Cover: Ruthertord-Appleton Laboratory; intro page and pages 5, 16 (r), 21 (t & l) and 31 (tr, bl & br): Science Photo Library; pages 7 (l), 8 (t), 9 (l), 16 (l), 17 (b) and back cover: Robert Harding Library; pages 7 (tr & br), 10 (both), 13 (t & b), 23 and 25 (both): Spectrum Colour Library; pages 7 (t), 14, 21 (r) and 31 (tl): Photosource; pages 8 (b), 18, 19 and 26 (b): Paul Brierley; pages 9 (t) and 13 (m): Zefa; page 9 (r): NASA; page 12: Hutchison Library; pages 15 and 26 (t): V. Bailey.